BUCKINGHAM
PALACE

BUCKINGHAM PALACE, which is today the principal state or official residence of the British Monarchy, has served that function only since comparatively recent times. In the Middle Ages the principal London residence of the Norman and Plantagenet kings and their successors was the Palace of Westminster, now rebuilt as the Houses of Parliament. Whitehall was the main royal palace from the reign of Henry VIII to that of William III when it was largely destroyed by fire. In the eighteenth century St James's Palace, built by Henry VIII on the site of a medieval leper hospital to serve as a hunting lodge, was used by the Hanoverian kings. The creation of Buckingham Palace as an appropriate symbol of national greatness in the aftermath of the victories of the Napoleonic Wars was due to George IV.

Although converted to a palace by George IV and first lived in by Queen Victoria soon after her accession in 1837, the property was acquired originally for the Crown by George III in 1761. The history of the site, however, can be traced back to the beginning of the seventeenth century and in 1633 Lord Goring built on it 'a fair house and other convenient buildings and outhouses'. In 1677 the Earl of Arlington rebuilt the house on a larger scale in the fashionable Caroline manner. The house was largely rebuilt yet again for John Sheffield, Duke of Buckingham, in 1702-5 by the architect William Winde.

The most attractive feature of the house was its setting between St James's and Hyde Parks, at the head of an avenue of limes and elms with views towards Westminster and the

City of London and with the dome of St Paul's visible in the distance. It was more a country house on the edge of London than a town house, and to some extent it has retained this character ever since.

Buckingham House remained the property of the Dukes of Buckingham – after whom it is named – until the mid-eighteenth century. A problem over the lease of the property, half of which was on Crown Land, enabled George III to acquire it in 1761 as a private residence following his marriage to Charlotte of Mecklenburg-Strelitz. Between 1762 and 1774 Buckingham House was remodelled at a cost of £73,000 by Sir William Chambers. The resulting house was a villa rather than a palace and emphatically a private residence of the royal family. The ceremonial centre of the court

TOP: *Buckingham House as it was in 1819. King George III simplified the façade of the Duke of Buckingham's house and added substantially to the north and south sides*

ABOVE: *An eighteenth-century view of St James's Park from Buckingham House showing the original forecourt. The tree-lined Mall is in the centre and Birdcage Walk on the right*

remained at St James's resulting in the anomaly whereby foreign ambassadors are still accredited to the Court of St James two centuries later.

The King's rooms at Buckingham House were fitted up neatly but, by royal standards, extremely plainly. The Queen's rooms were far more richly furnished and were filled with her collections of china, ivories, snuff-boxes, etuis, jade, lacquer and pretty *objets de vertu*. The old two-storey Saloon of Buckingham House was completely redecorated and served as the Queen's throne room later in the reign when she started holding her 'drawing-rooms' there rather than at St James's.

In the last years of his reign George III spent more time at Windsor and Kew than in London, but Queen Charlotte continued to use the Queen's House till her death in 1818. The house then lay empty until the accession to the throne of George IV in 1820.

His first idea was to remodel it as a private residence for use in conjunction with St James's, as in his father's day, but by 1826 he decided to convert it into a palatial residence where he could hold his courts and con-duct the official business of the monarchy.

He chose as his architect John Nash whose design for the new palace was theatrical and fran-cophile, perfectly reflecting George IV's personal taste. Nash was ham-pered, however, by the ambivalence of intention over the purpose of the palace – as to whether it was to be a private royal residence or a state palace – as well as by chronic short-age of funds. He was thus forced to keep and remodel the old house. To this day the shell of the Duke of Buckingham's and George III's house is still incorporated in the middle of the principal range of the palace. It dictates the plan and

Allan Ramsay: George III, 1761

dimensions of the rooms and the proportions of the ground floor.

Nevertheless, Nash's plan was an ingenious solution to a difficult architectural problem. The main block was doubled in size by the addition of new rooms on the garden side; the old wings were demolished and replaced by new ones to form a solid u-shape enclos-ing an open courtyard, the fourth side of which was finished with iron railings and a central triumphal arch, commemorating the victories of Trafalgar and Waterloo (nick-named the Marble Arch, it is now at the north-east corner of Hyde Park). The old main block was remodelled, permitting both a circuit of the State Rooms and an axial approach to the Throne Room within the shell of the Duke of Buckingham's house.

Queen Charlotte at the age of twenty-one, at her dressing table in Buckingham House. She is seated with George, Prince of Wales, in Roman costume, and Frederick, later Duke of York, in Turkish robes. Painted by Johann Zoffany in 1764

Buckingham Palace showing the Marble Arch in its original position at the entrance to the forecourt. A watercolour by Joseph Nash, 1846

This made the new state rooms on the first floor equally suitable for formal audiences and for more social court events.

The exterior of Nash's palace, faced in Bath stone, is exquisitely detailed in a French Neo-classical manner expressive of George IV's personal taste and making much use of sculptured panels and trophies, while the main feature of the garden front was a domed semi-circular bow.

The interiors of the palace were progressively enriched by George IV with the advice of his artistic 'guru' Sir Charles Long, to meet an increasing desire for opulence and grandeur. The decoration was notable for its large-scale use of brightly coloured scagliola, lapis blue and raspberry pink, the use of sculptured plaster panels set high up, and elaborately decorated ceilings.

The Blue, White and Green Drawing Rooms, the Music Room and Throne Room are among the most original as well as the most opulent state rooms of their date. The Picture Gallery in the middle with its classical hammer beam roof, influenced perhaps by Soane, was less successful, and despite its ingenuity, failed to throw light on the pictures, with the result that it has since been remodelled.

The completion of the palace was entrusted by William IV to Edward Blore, a more competent but far less inspired architect. In general he kept to the lines of Nash's design, but made it more solid and less picturesque by smoothing out the projections and removing the much criticised dome and 'turrets' from the roof line.

William IV never lived in Buckingham Palace, though it was completed in his reign. In 1837, when Queen Victoria moved in, the Palace was fresh from the hands of the builders. The inadequacies of the new palace became obvious following the Queen's marriage to her cousin, Prince Albert of Saxe-Coburg, in 1840. The root of the trouble was that the palace was too small, both for state functions and for family life. Splendid though

George IV's state apartments were, none of them was big enough for a court ball. Equally serious for the newly married couple was the absence of any nurseries. Moreover, there were not enough bedrooms for visitors, and the kitchens were old-fashioned and badly planned. The obvious solution was to make the palace a complete quadrangle by closing the east side of the courtyard with a new wing. This scheme was adopted and entailed the removal of the Marble Arch; it was in any case too narrow for the state coach to pass through, a result of Nash's slapdash methods of designing.

The new range, with the necessary apartments for distinguished visitors on the first floor and nurseries on top, was designed by Edward Blore and built by Thomas Cubitt from 1847 to 1850. Blore's new front made no effort to relate either stylistically or in its material to Nash's original architecture and thus spoilt the unity of George IV's palace.

The extension of the suite of state apartments along the west front of the palace by the addition at the south end of new galleries, a State Supper Room and a huge Ballroom, 123 feet long and 60 feet wide, was entrusted to a different architect, Nash's pupil, James Pennethorne.

In the later years of her reign, Queen Victoria spent more time at Windsor Castle, and Buckingham Palace remained dark and shuttered up for most of the year. When Edward VII came to the throne in 1901, it seemed dingy and old-fashioned and he considered the redecoration of the palace 'a duty and necessity' before he moved in two years later. The Ballroom, Grand Entrance, Marble Hall, Grand

Sir George Hayter: The Coronation of Queen Victoria, *1838*

Staircase, vestibules and galleries were all painted white, heavily gilded, and embellished with finicky festoons, swags and other decorative motifs at odds with Nash's original detailing.

Some atonement for these alterations was made by the work carried out at Buckingham Palace under George V and Queen Mary. Blore had used soft Caen stone for the east range which proved to be perishable in the London climate. It was, therefore, decided in 1913 to re-face the Blore front in Portland stone to a new design by Aston Webb as a backdrop to the Queen Victoria Memorial and the culmination of the remodelled approach along the Mall, planned in 1901.

It is due to Webb that Buckingham Palace looks like everybody's idea of a palace. Much of the architectural effect comes from the forecourt and new *rond point* in front, with magnificent gateways and railings, the gilded ironwork of which was made by the Bromsgrove Guild.

Queen Mary took a keen personal interest in the interiors of all the royal palaces and initiated many improvements and schemes of restoration. Perhaps her greatest contribution to Buckingham Palace was the rearrangement and restoration of historic contents, reassembling sets of chairs, for instance, which had been split up. The informed and historically accurate approach, initiated by Queen Mary,

TOP: *The Royal Family on the balcony*

ABOVE: *The Centre Room, from which members of the Royal Family emerge to wave from the balcony to the crowds after ceremonial occasions*

The fly-past at The Queen's Official Birthday

has conditioned the upkeep and presentation of the royal residences and their contents down to the present.

Today The Queen and the Duke of Edinburgh live in the private apartments on the north side of the palace; rooms on the upper floors of the north and east sides are occupied by other members of the royal family. Much of the ground floor and the south wing are occupied by household officers and service quarters. The principal rooms, which, form the backdrop to the pageantry of court ceremonial and official entertaining, occupy the main west block facing the gardens. In all, Buckingham Palace has 19 state rooms, 52 royal and guest bedrooms, 188 staff bedrooms, 92 offices and 78 bathrooms. Some 450 people work in the palace and 40,000 people are entertained there every year.

Unlike many other historic monuments, Buckingham Palace remains a fully occupied, working royal palace and this gives it a particular fascination. The Queen, as head of state, receives there a large number of formal and informal visitors, including the Prime Minister at weekly audiences, the Privy Council, foreign and British ambassadors and high commissioners, bishops and senior officers of the armed services and the civil service. There are regular investitures in the Ballroom. Each autumn the Queen gives a splendid formal reception in the state rooms for all the diplomatic corps in London. Three times a year, in the summer, garden parties are held which are attended by a wide range of guests including MPs, clergy and those active in local and public life, amounting to 27,000 people in all. The practice of holding small, private lunch parties for guests drawn from leaders in the community is an innovation of the present reign.

The highlight of royal entertaining, however, is the state banquet, usually for about 170 guests, given by The Queen on the first evening of a state visit of a foreign head of state to the United Kingdom. At Buckingham Palace, state banquets are held in the Ballroom, the largest of the state rooms, using the magnificent gold plate from the Royal Collection, much of it made for George IV. Guests are received in the Music Room and after they have taken their places at table, a royal procession is formed to the Ballroom, led by The Queen and the visiting head of state and preceded by the Lord Chamberlain and the Lord Steward who both walk backwards.

The Lord Chamberlain is the head of the whole household, responsible for the running of the palace and organization of the court ceremonial, as well as the upkeep of the palace and its collections. Under him are the heads of various departments, which include the Crown Equerry, in charge of the Mews, the Keeper of the Privy Purse and the Master of the Household, a position dating back to 1539. The latter is in charge of the domestic and staff arrangements, as well as catering and official entertaining. His department of 195 people is one of the largest in the Royal Household. This complex organization is run with clockwork precision and maintains the high standards of traditional hospitality and faultless ceremonial that have been admired features of the English royal palaces since the Middle Ages.

VISITORS ENTER the Palace from Buckingham Gate through the Amabassadors' Court.

The Ambassadors' Entrance is a temple-like Ionic portico of Bath stone on the south side of the Palace. It was added under the direction of Edward Blore after Nash had been dismissed as architect of the palace in 1830, but takes its cue from the Nash conservatories on the garden front (one of which is now the Queen's Gallery with changing exhibitions from the Royal Collection). This is the entrance used on official occasions by the diplomats and others with the privilege of entrée. The hall itself is a narrow space, known as the Entrée, lined with marbled pilasters, while the gilded ceiling is a modest overture to the glories to come. The Brocatello chimneypiece with the mirror over it are insertions in the seventeenth-century style when the Entrée was redecorated in 1924 and bear the monogram of King George V. The mirror incoporates a gilded sunburst clock, its dial encircled by the Garter bearing the motto 'Honi soit qui mal y pense'. Portraits of the early Hanoverian monarchs line the walls, leading to the glazed doors to the Quadrangle.

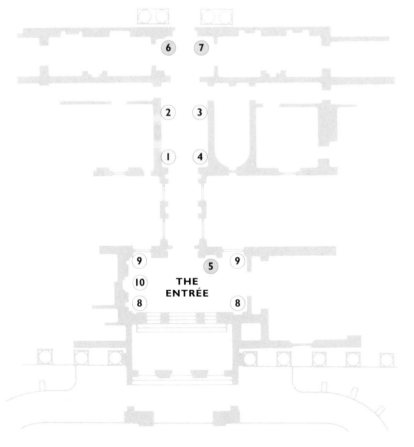

PICTURES

1 John Shackleton: *George II*, 1757

2 George Wilhelm Fountaine: *George I*, c. 1725

3 Sir George Hayter: *Queen Victoria*, c. 1840

4 Anonymous, British School, *Frederick, Prince of Wales*, c. 1745

SCULPTURE

5 John McCombe Reynolds, bronze bust of H. M. The Queen, 1984

6 Sir Francis Chantrey, *Arthur, 1st Duke of Wellington*, 1837

7 E. Davis, *Victoria, Duchess of Kent*, 1843

FURNITURE

8 Pair of French patinated and gilt bronze candelabra, late 18th century; on English giltwood tripod torchères, early 19th century

9 Pair of Chinese celadon vases with gilt bronze mounts attributed to the Vulliamys, c. 1810

10 Cistern, Spode porcelain, with gilt bronze mounts attibuted to Benjamin Lewis Vulliamy, c. 1820

In the Quadrangle the visitor first savours the impact of Nash's architecture for King George IV. Here all seems to be golden Bath stone, but Blore's surviving rear elevation of the east range is actually stuccoed and painted stone colour, while the lower columns are of cast iron, also painted. The quality of George IV's conception is apparent in the large but elegant double portico with its superimposed columns, stoutly Doric at ground floor level and richly Corinthian above, influenced by Claude Perrault's design for the Louvre portico in Paris.

An important feature of the original design of Buckingham Palace was the programme of integrated sculptural ornament intended to display contemporary artistic talent and reflecting the early nineteenth-century enthusiasm for British art, as manifested also in the array of marble monuments to national heroes in St Paul's Cathedral. John Flaxman, the greatest of English Neo-classical sculptors, was first approached to design the carved decorations. But he died in 1826 after making sketches for the external sculpture which was executed by other hands. The beautifully moulded capitals and friezes are of Coade stone (a type of terracotta invented in the eighteenth century by Mrs Elizabeth Coade), supplied by William Croggan in 1827.

Croggan also made the crowning figures of *Neptune, Commerce* and *Navigation*. In the pediment is a relief, dated 1828, by E. H. Baily depicting *Britannia Acclaimed by Neptune*. Inside the portico is a relief with seven roundels showing the *Progress of Navigation* by J. E. Carew. The original scheme for this entrance sculpture was British sea power and maritime trade. The two panels incorporated by Blore in the attic storey are by Richard Westmacott and were originally intended for the Marble Arch. They celebrate the Battle of Trafalgar (*The Death of Nelson*) and the Battle of Waterloo (*The Meeting of Blücher and Wellington*).

THE GRAND HALL is of the same dimensions as the hall of the old Buckingham House and retains the same low proportions stressing that this is the sub-storey with the main rooms up above on a *piano nobile*, as in an Italian Renaissance palace. Nash created dramatic spatial effects by lowering the floor of the central area. There are interesting vistas across the different levels into the adjoining spaces, and agreeable contrasts of light and shade. The spatial qualities of the room are enhanced by the use of rich materials. The floor and Corinthian columns are all of white Carrara marble, supplied by Joseph Browne who was sent to Italy by Nash to procure the marble used in the decoration of the palace. The Corinthian capitals are of gilded bronze supplied by Samuel Parker. The chimney-piece at the north end of the hall, facing the Grand Staircase, is among the finest in the palace and was supplied in 1829, at a cost of £1,000, by Joseph Theakston, 'the ablest carver of his time'. Its design shows the influence of Napoleon's architects Percier and Fontaine. At the top is a small bust of George IV, a comparatively modest 'signature' for the chief creator of Buckingham Palace. Originally the marmoreal quality of this hall was enhanced by the treatment of the walls which were entirely lined with coloured scagliola. The present white and gold decoration was executed in 1902 by C. H. Bessant for Edward VII.

The spatial complexity of the hall is continued in the Grand Staircase where Nash contrived an almost Baroque vista, the steps continuing in one straight flight from the half-landing as well as returning in two arms along the sides. It provides a dramatic transition to the state rooms on the first floor. Light floods down from the engraved glass skylights by Wainwright and Brothers, the patterns on which are reminiscent of white damask tablecloths.

The staircase, of Carrara marble, replaces James Wyatt's imperial staircase of 1801 for George III. The sumptuous gilt bronze balustrade embellished with rich Grecian foliage is reflected in the design of the plaster string-course round the walls. It was made by Samuel Parker in 1828–30 and is the finest of its type in England. It cost £3,900. Parker also provided the gilt metal mounts for the unique mahogany framed mirror-plated doors designed by Nash and used throughout the state rooms, adding enormously to their glittery spaciousness. He charged 7d each for 'the little fleurs de lys' mouldings. The walls, which are now white and gold, were originally covered with polychrome panels of scagliola. The sculptural decoration in moulded plaster survives and was influenced by Percier and Fontaine's palace interiors for Napoleon. Here they were designed by the painter Thomas Stothard. The long rectangular reliefs of the four seasons were executed by his son Alfred Stothard, while the reliefs of cupids in the lunettes were modelled by Francis Bernasconi, the leading plasterer at the palace.

State Ball at Buckingham Palace, 5 July 1848. *Eugène Lami's watercolour shows Nash's Grand Staircase of the late 1820s with its balustrade by Samuel Parker and Gruner's polychrome wall decoration of 1845*

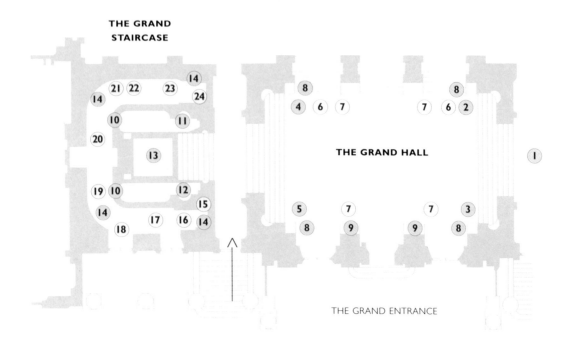

THE GRAND STAIRCASE

THE GRAND HALL

THE GRAND ENTRANCE

THE GRAND HALL

SCULPTURE

1 Chimney-piece and overmantel by Joseph Theakston, 1829

2 Richard James Wyatt: *Nymph of Diana*, c.1850; completed by John Gibson and Benjamin Edward Spence after Wyatt's death

3 Wolf von Hoyer: *Psyche with a Lamp*, 1851

4 Pietro Tenerani: *Flora*, 1848

5 William Theed: *Psyche Lamenting the Loss of Cupid*, 1847

FURNITURE

6 Set of hall chairs and settees made by Elward, Marsh & Tatham, mahogany painted with Prince of Wales feathers, 1802; made for the Hall at the Royal Pavilion, Brighton

7 Set of chairs, mahogany and gilt with tapering backs, painted with Queen Victoria's cypher, c.1790; made for the Hall at Carlton House, London

PORCELAIN

8 Set of four cisterns, Spode porcelain, with gilt bronze mounts attributed to Benjamin Louis Vulliamy, c.1820

9 Pair of dark blue Chinese porcelain vases with French gilt bronze mounts, c.1765

THE GRAND STAIRCASE

FITTINGS

10 Balustrade supplied by Samuel Parker, 1828-30, at a cost of £3,900.

SCULPTURE

11 Jan Geefs: *Love and Malice*, 1859; birthday present from Queen Victoria to Prince Albert, 26 August 1859

12 Richard James Wyatt: *The Huntress*, 1850; birthday present from Queen Victoria to Prince Albert, 26 August 1850

13 Bronze 19th-century copy of Benvenuto Cellini's *Perseus and Medusa* in the Loggia dei Lanzi, Florence

PORCELAIN

14 Four Chinese porcelain vases with gilt bronze mounts, early 19th century; they may have been the four large china bottles with swan head mounts purchased by George IV from the dealer Robert Fogg in 1823 for £520

PICTURES

Portraits of Queen Victoria's immediate ancestors and relations, illustrating her succession; an installation devised for Queen Victoria shortly after her Coronation in 1838.

15 Sir Thomas Lawrence: *William IV*, 1827

16 Sir Thomas Lawrence: *Prince George of Cumberland* (later George V, King of Hanover), 1828

17 After George Dawe: *Princess Charlotte of Wales*, c.1817

18 After George Dawe: *Leopold I, King of the Belgians*, 1844

19 Sir William Beechey: *Queen Charlotte*, 1796

20 Sir William Beechey: *George III*, 1799-1800

21 Sir George Hayter: *Victoria, Duchess of Kent*, 1835

22 Sir David Wilkie: *Augustus, Duke of Sussex*, 1833

23 George Dawe: *Edward, Duke of Kent*, 1818

24 Sir Martin Archer Shee: *Queen Adelaide*, 1836

THE NEXT THREE ROOMS extending along the courtyard side of the palace form a shortened version of the traditional sequence in English palaces, still to be seen at its full extent in the Wren state rooms at Hampton Court.

Because of lack of space at Buckingham Palace, the Guard Room is a mere formality and too small to accommodate the ceremonial guards on formal occasions. They are deployed instead in the adjoining rooms. The guards are composed of two corps of the Yeomen of the Guard, the royal bodyguard, initiated by Henry VII in 1485, and are the oldest in the world; they still wear picturesque Tudor uniform. The other is the Gentlemen-at-Arms founded by Henry VIII in 1537, who wear magnificent scarlet and gold nineteenth-century pattern uniforms with plumed helmets of polished steel.

The Guard Room makes up for its comparatively small size with lavish decoration. It is pure Nash, with apsidal ends and engraved glass ceiling lights by Wainright and Brothers. The plaster reliefs of *War and Peace* are by William Pitts (1790-1840), who designed and modelled most of the high relief plasterwork in the state rooms. He started life as a silver chaser and modeller and executed the famous silver-gilt 'Achilles Shield' to Flaxman's design. His work at Buckingham Palace has considerable grace and charm but is perhaps too small in scale to be fully appreciated in its lofty situation.

GUESTS, OFFICIAL GROUPS and delegations gather here before proceeding to the Throne Room or Music Room to meet their hosts. This room occupies the site of Queen Charlotte's Saloon and retains to a large extent the original character of the Nash architecture with green silk wall hangings framed by the plasterer George Jackson's lattice patterned pilasters. The original silk (now replaced) was woven in Ireland at Queen Adelaide's request to provide employment there.

The ceiling is the first of a series of extraordinary designs by Nash with domes and concave and convex coving, which develops the tent-like 'Mogul' themes originally explored by him at the Royal Pavilion, Brighton; they are a unique feature of the state rooms at Buckingham Palace. *Fraser's Magazine* in 1830 wrote, 'It is indeed, not easy to conceive anything more splendid than the designs for ceilings which are to be finished in a style new in this country, partaking very much of the boldest style in the Italian taste of the fifteenth century … they will present the effect of embossed gold ornaments'. The details and motifs are derived from a wide range of sources including the Italian Renaissance as well as Classical Greece and Rome; they stretch the canon of Georgian taste to the limits. The carved marble chimney-pieces are part of a series supplied for the palace by Joseph Browne at a cost of £6,000 between 1827 and 1830.

ABOVE: *Sèvres porcelain potpourri vase,1758, which may have belonged to Madame de Pompadour, Louis XV's mistress*

BELOW: *French chest of drawers by Martin Carlin, c.1775. The pietre dure panels are about one hundred years earlier in date*

THE THRONE ROOM, 60 feet long, is dominated by the almost Baroque 'proscenium' flanked by a pair of lively winged genii holding gilded garlands above the 'chairs of state'; the genii are Bernasconi's masterpiece. The plaster frieze, designed by Thomas Stothard, is remarkable for its attempt to treat a medieval subject – the Wars of the Roses – as if it were the Parthenon frieze. It is only the Gothic armour that gives the game away. The subjects are the *Battle of Tewkesbury* (north), *Marriage of Henry VII and Elizabeth of York* (east), the *Battle of Bosworth* (west), *Bellona, Goddess of War, Encouraging the Troops* (south). The same attempt to assimilate medieval ideas in Classical dress enlivens the bold display of heraldry of the four kingdoms of England, Scotland, Ireland and Hanover, and Garter stars, on the plaster cove. The elaborate doorcase opposite the throne is of scagliola (now painted) and was made by William Croggan; the little bust of William IV above shows that the decoration of this room was completed to the Nash designs after George IV's death. The crimson silk hangings on the walls are a recent restoration. The four carved and gilt trophies on either side of the throne may have come from Carlton House.

THE GUARD ROOM
THE GREEN DRAWING ROOM

THE GUARD ROOM

TAPESTRIES

1 Two Gobelins tapestries, 18th century; from the series *Les Portières des Dieux: Venus Symbolising Spring* (left); *Bacchus Symbolising Autumn* (right)

SCULPTURE

2 John Gibson: *Queen Victoria*, 1847; originally partly tinted

3 Emil Wolff: *Prince Albert*, 1846; a replica of the original now at Osborne House, Isle of Wight. The Prince is dressed in Roman costume

4 Mary Thornycroft: *Princesses Victoria and Maud of Wales*, 1877

5 Benjamin Edward Spence: *Lady of the Lake*, 1861; birthday present from Queen Victoria to Prince Albert, 26 August 1861

6 Benjamin Edward Spence: *Highland Mary*, 1853; birthday present from Prince Albert to Queen Victoria, 24 May 1853

7 Mary Thornycroft: *Princess Louise of Wales*, 1877

FURNITURE

8 Set of seats by Morel & Seddon, 1826-28; made for Windsor Castle

9 Chandelier, probably supplied by Parker & Perry, c. 1811, for Carlton House, London

THE GREEN DRAWING ROOM

PICTURES

10 Studio of Allan Ramsay: *Augusta, Princess of Wales*, c. 1764

11 German School: *Frederick Henry, Charles Louis and Elizabeth* (children of Frederick V and Elizabeth, King and Queen of Bohemia), c. 1620

12 Nathaniel Dance: *Edward Augustus, Duke of York* (brother of George III), 1764

13 John Michael Wright: *James, Duke of Cambridge* (son of James II and his first wife Anne Hyde), 1666-7

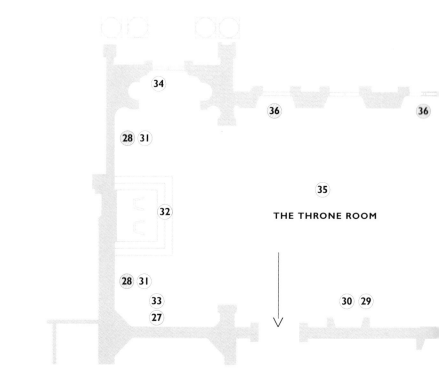

THE THRONE ROOM

14 Francis Cotes: *Princesses Louisa Ann and Caroline Matilda* (later Queen of Denmark, sisters of George III), 1767

15 Sofonisba Anguissola (attrib.): *Isabella Clara Eugenia and Catharina* (daughters of Philip II, King of Spain), c. 1569-70

16 Sir Martin Archer Shee: *Richard, Marquess Wellesley*, (brother of the 1st Duke of Wellington, when Lord Steward of the Household), c.1832

FURNITURE

17 Grand piano with six octave action by Isaac Mott, 1817; purchased by George IV in 1820 for £238 5s, it was placed in the Music Room Gallery at the Royal Pavilion, Brighton, together with the music stool

18 Four semi-circular pedestals, gilded wood, c. 1790; probably made in England to a French design for the Throne Room, Carlton House, London. They support gilt and patinated bronze French Empire candelabra

19 Set of seats by Morel & Seddon, 1826-28; made for Windsor Castle

20 Chest of drawers by Martin Carlin, ebony and gilt bronze, c. 1775. The raised *pietre dure*

panels are about 100 years earlier in date; two have scratched on the back the name Gian Ambrogio Giachetti who was employed by Louis XIV at the Gobelins manufactory to make mosaic panels. Bought by George IV in 1828, it had previously belonged to the singer Marie-Joséphine Laguerre

21 Cabinet by Adam Weisweiler, veneered with Boulle marquetry with gilt bronze mounts, c. 1780-85. It is enriched with 17th-century panels of *pietra dura*; some, such as the two with single flowers, may have been made in Florence and those in relief at the Gobelins manufactory. Probably bought by George IV for Carlton House, London, in 1791

THE QUADRANGLE

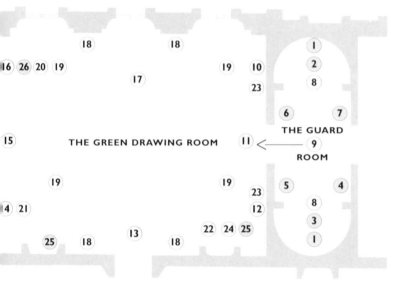

THE GREEN DRAWING ROOM

THE GUARD ROOM

22 Pair of four-light candelabra by Benjamin Lewis Vulliamy, gilt and patinated bronze in the form of three female figures standing back to back, 1811; their design is inspired by the French Empire style

23 Two French cabinets on later stands, veneered with tortoise-shell, pewter and ebony in *prèmiere-* and *contre-partie* marquetry (pewter on tortoiseshell and tortoiseshell on pewter), late 17th-early 18th century

24 French Empire clock with a figure of Apollo probably designed by Martin-Eloi Lignereux with mounts supplied by Pierre-Philippe Thomire, 1803; bought by George IV in 1803

PORCELAIN

25 All the ornamental porcelain vases are of soft-paste Sèvres; these pieces and the others in the State Apartments form part of the collection assembled by George IV, now principally in Buckingham Palace and Windsor Castle

26 Potpourri vase, soft-paste Sèvres porcelain in the form of a ship, 1758; it probably belonged to Madame de Pompadour and was purchased by George IV in 1817

THE THRONE ROOM

PICTURES

27 Angelica Kauffmann: *Augusta, Duchess of Brunswick, with her son Charles* (sister of George III and mother of Queen Caroline, consort of George IV), 1767

SCULPTURE

28 Four trophies, gilded wood, *c.* 1795, said to have come from the Old Throne Room, Carlton House, London

FURNITURE

29 'Oath of the Horatii' Clock by Claude Galle, early 19th century; based on the painting by Louis David, 1784. Bought by George IV in 1809

30 Pair of candelabra attributed to Claude Galle, gilt and patinated bronze in the form of cornucopia, early 19th century; purchased by George IV in 1814

31 Pair of Council Chairs by Tatham, Bailey & Sanders, 1812; supplied for George IV at Carlton House, London

32 Throne chairs of H.M. The Queen and the Duke of Edinburgh. by White, Allom & Co; made for the Coronation ceremony of 1953

33 Throne chairs of King George VI and Queen Elizabeth by White, Allom & Co; used during part of the Coronation ceremony of 1937

34 Throne chair of Queen Victoria by Thomas Dowbiggin, 1837

35 Chandeliers, cut glass and gilt bronze, *c.* 1810; probably from Carlton House, London

PORCELAIN

36 Pair of Chinese porcelain jardinières, early 18th century; the gilt bronze mounts are attributed to Benjamin Lewis Vulliamy, *c.* 1820

The Picture Gallery (TOP) *as it is today* (ABOVE) *and in 1843, a watercolour by Douglas Morison showing Prince Albert's arrangement of the pictures*

THIS IS THE GREAT SPINE of the state apartments. It is 155 feet long and is entirely top lit. It occupies the site of the first floor rooms of old Buckingham House. It was designed by Nash to display George IV's outstanding collection of Dutch and Flemish paintings, many of which still hang here. The original ceiling was a complex design combining a timber hammer beam frame with hanging pendants and a series of 17 little glazed saucer domes or lanterns. It was something of a practical failure as it leaked and failed to throw light on the pictures. It was modified by Blore and totally remodelled for George V in 1914 as a glazed segmental arched ceiling. The doorcases were also simplified and the columnar screen at the south end redesigned. The architect for these changes was Frank Baines, chief architect of the Office of Works. The wood carvings in the style of Grinling Gibbons, were made by H. H. Martyn of Cheltenham. The result is rather like the interior of the saloon of one of the great ocean liners of this period. Its 'subdued tastefulness' makes a striking contrast to the extreme opulence of Nash's adjoining rooms. The walls were hung in 1914 with olive green silk damask woven by Warners, but this has since been replaced by the present light pink-beige coverings.

The four Carrara marble chimney-pieces supplied by Joseph Browne in the 1820s survive from the gallery's first incarnation and were designed by Nash. They each display a circular portrait relief of a famous artist: Dürer, Van Dyck, Titian and Leonardo. It is the quality of the paintings, however, which makes this room so remarkable: the collection includes works by Rubens and Rembrandt, van Dyck and Vermeer.

ABOVE: *Sir Anthony van Dyck: Charles I, 1633*

RIGHT: *One of a pair of black Sèvres porcelain vases, c. 1790*

FACING PAGE

TOP LEFT: *One of two pedestals by Gilles Joubert, made in 1762 originally to support clocks giving solar and lunar time. They now support 18th-century bronze busts of the Emperors Augustus (shown here) and Vespasian*

TOP RIGHT: *Rembrandt van Rijn:* Agatha Bas, 1641

BOTTOM LEFT: *Sir Peter Paul Rubens:* Milkmaids with Cattle in a Landscape ('The Farm at Laeken'), *c. 1617-18*

BOTTOM RIGHT: *Guercino:* The Libyan Sibyl, *c. 1651*

THIS PAGE

ABOVE: *One of a pair of Japanese lacquer bowls with French gilt bronze mounts, mid-18th century*

BELOW: *Aelbert Cuyp:* Landscape with a Negro Page, *c. 1655*

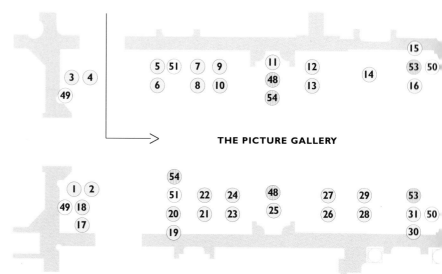

THE THRONE ROOM

THE PICTURE GALLERY

THE WHITE DRAWING ROOM

PICTURES

The arrangement of pictures has changed over the years. Most of the paintings now in the Picture Gallery were acquired either by Charles I, Frederick, Prince of Wales, George III or, principally, George IV. Outstanding works are marked with an asterisk.

1 Guido Reni: *Cleopatra, c. 1630**

2 Gonzales Coques: *Family of Jan-Baptista Anthoine,* copper, 1664

3 Guercino: *The Libyan Sibyl, c. 1651**

4 Barent Graat: *A Family Group,* 1658

5 David Teniers the Younger: *The Stolen Kiss, c. 1640*

6 Rembrandt van Rijn: *Noli me tangere (Christ and the Magdalen at the Tomb),* panel, 1638*

7 Sir Anthony van Dyck: *Virgin and Child, c. 1630-2*

8 Aelbert Cuyp: *The Passage Boat, c.1650**

9 Nicholaes Berchem: *A Mountainous Landscape with Herdsmen Driving Cattle down a Road,* 1673

10 Circle of Frans Hals: *Standing Cavalier, c. 1630*

11 Francesco Zuccarelli: *Landscape with Two Young Children Offering Fruit to a Woman, c. 1743*

12 David Teniers the Younger: *Fishermen on the Seashore, c. 1660*

13 Sir Anthony van Dyck: *Zeger van Hontsum, c. 1630*

14 Ferdinand Bol (attrib.): *Rembrandt van Rijn and his Wife, Saskia,* 1640-50

15 Aelbert Cuyp: *Cows in a Pasture beside a River before the Ruins of the Abbey of Rijnsburg.,* 1640-50

16 Rembrandt van Rijn: *Agatha Bas, 1641**

17 Nicolaes Maes: *The Listening Housewife,* 1655

18 Gabriel Metsu: *The Cello Player, c. 1665*

19 Philips Wouwermans: *The Hayfield, c. 1660*

20 Sir Peter Paul Rubens: *The Assumption of the Virgin,* panel, c. 1611*

21 Sir Anthony van Dyck: *The Mystic Marriage of St Catherine, c. 1630**

22 Sir Peter Paul Rubens: *Milkmaids with Cattle in a Landscape ('The Farm at Laeken'),* panel, c. 1617-18*

23 Philips Wouwermans: *A Horse Fair in front of a Town, c. 1660*

24 Isaac van Ostade (attrib.): *Girl Crossing a Brook, c. 1635*

25 Francesco Zuccarelli: *Landscape with Two Seated Women Embracing, c. 1743*

26 Domenico Fetti: *Vincenzo Avogadro, c. 1620*

27 Willem van de Velde the Younger: *A Calm: A States Yacht under Sail, close to the Shore, and Many Other Vessels,* panel, c. 1655*

28 Aelbert Cuyp: *A Cavalry Trooper Decorating his Dappled Grey Horse, c. 1655*

29 David Teniers the Younger: *Peasants Dancing outside a Country House,* panel, 1645

30 Carlo Dolci: *Salome with the Head of St John the Baptist,* 1660-70

31 Willem van de Velde the Younger: *'The Golden Leeuw' at Sea in Heavy Weather, c. 1671*

32 Sir Anthony van Dyck: *Charles I and Henrietta Maria with their two Eldest Children ('The Greate Peece'), 1632**

33 Canaletto: *Venice: The Piazzetta towards the Torre dell'Orologio, c. 1728**

34 Luca Carlevaris: *A Caprice Landscape with a Fountain and an Artist Sketching, c. 1710*

35 Gaspar Poussin: *Jonah and the Whale, c. 1653-4*

36 Melchior de Hondecoeter: *Birds and a Spaniel, c. 1665*

37 Sir Peter Paul Rubens: *Landscape with St George and the Dragon, c. 1630*

38 Luca Carlevaris: *A Caprice View of a Seaport, c. 1710*

39 Claude Lorrain: *The Rape of Europa, 1667**

40 Sir Anthony van Dyck: *Charles I with M. de St Antoine, 1633**

41 Canaletto: *Venice: Piazza S. Marco from a Corner of the Basilica, 1728**

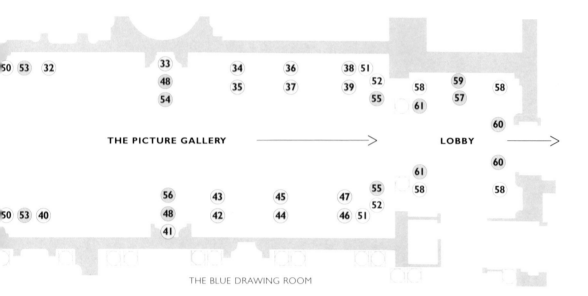

THE PICTURE GALLERY ⟶

LOBBY ⟶

THE BLUE DRAWING ROOM

42 Luca Carlevaris: *A Caprice View with a Shipyard,* c. 1710

43 Gaspar Poussin: *Landscape with a Waterfall,* c. 1653-4

44 Jan Steen: *A Village Revel,* 1673

45 Aelbert Cuyp: *Landscape with a Negro Page,* c. 1655*

46 Luca Carlevaris: *A Caprice View of a Harbour,* c. 1710

47 Gaspar Poussin: *Landscape with Figures by a Pool,* c. 1665

FITTINGS

48 Chimney-pieces supplied by Joseph Browne and almost certainly carved by Italian sculptors, late 1820s; they incorporate busts of Titian, Dürer, van Dyck and Leonardo da Vinci

FURNITURE

49 Pair of cabinets by Pierre Garnier, veneered with ebony and inlaid with panels of pewter, tortoise-shell and brass, c. 1770; bought for George IV in Paris in 1819

50 Four armchairs by Georges Jacob, c. 1786; imported into England by Dominique Daguerre in the late 1780s, they were placed in the Prince's bedroom at Carlton House, London

51 Set of four French console tables attributed to Adam Weisweiler; marble-topped and veneered with tulipwood, c. 1785; the gilt bronze scrollwork, was added by Benjamin Vulliamy in 1811

52 Two pedestals supplied by Gilles Joubert, veneered with trellis marquetry in kingwood and tulipwood, 1762. Made to support clocks giving solar and lunar time, they originally stood on either side of the alcove in Louis XV's bedroom at Versailles, but now support 18th-century bronze busts of the Emperors Augustus and Vespasian. Acquired by George IV in 1818

PORCELAIN AND LACQUER

53 Japanese lacquer bowls with French gilt bronze mounts in the Louis XV and Louis XVI styles, 18th century

54 Two pairs of vases, hard-paste Sèvres porcelain painted in platinum and gold on a black ground with chinoiserie scenes and with gilt bronze mounts, c. 1790-92; and another pair, un-decorated, with siren mounts, c. 1786

55 Pair of jardinières, cloisonné enamel on gilded wood stands, 19th century

56 Pair of 'lac burgauté' vases, with gilt bronze mounts, attributed to the Vulliamys, early 19th century

THE PICTURE GALLERY LOBBY

SCULPTURE

57 Sir Francis Chantrey: *Mrs Jordan and Two Children,* 1834; commissioned by William IV after her death. The group was bequeathed to H.M. The Queen by the Earl of Munster in 1975

FURNITURE

58 Set of lyre-backed chairs, part gilded, probably made for Carlton House by François Hervé, c. 1790

EMBROIDERY

59 Large Italian needlework panel, representing the *Annunciation* within an arabesque border, mid-17th century

PORCELAIN

60 Pair of large octagonal Chinese porcelain vases, late 18th century

61 Pair of large celadon vases in the form of ewers with French gilt bronze mounts, early 19th century

THESE LESSER PASSAGE ROOMS act as ante-rooms or links between the Nash state rooms and the block added to the west by Pennethorne in 1853-5, to provide space for Queen Victoria's vast new ballroom. They all contain fine furniture, sculpture and paintings but do not match the originality and splendour of Nash's rooms. Traces of the original decorations conceived under Prince Albert's direction can be seen in the East and West galleries, including grisaille panels of *Cupids at Play* by Nicolà Consoni under the direction of Ludwig Gruner.

Studio of Sir Peter Paul Rubens: The Family of Balthasar Gerbier, *c. 1630*

One of four tapestries woven at the Gobelins manufactory from a series of twenty-eight illustrating the exploits of Don Quixote, second half of the 18th century, given to George IV by the artist Richard Cosway

THE QUADRANGLE

THE EAST GALLERY

THE SILK
TAPESTRY ROOM

THE
CROSS

GALLERY

THE STATE DINING ROOM

THE WEST GALLERY

THE SILK TAPESTRY ROOM

PICTURES

1 Francesco Zuccarelli: *River Landscape with the Finding of Moses*, 1768

2 Allan Ramsay: *Queen Charlotte with her Two Eldest Children*, 1764

3 Benjamin West: *The Apotheosis of Prince Octavius*, 1783

SCULPTURE

4 Bronze reduction of the equestrian statue of *Louis XV* after Edmé Bouchardon, which was unveiled in 1763 in the Place Louis XV (now Place de la Concorde), Paris; this reduction is probably one of seven cast by Louis-Claude Vassé, *c.* 1764

FURNITURE

5 French chest of drawers attributed to Adam Weisweiler, mahogany-veneered, late 18th century

6 Table by Morel & Seddon, ebony with *pietra dura* slab and gilt bronze mounts, raised on four pairs of gilded wood supports, *c.* 1828; made for Windsor Castle

7 Side table by Adam Weisweiler, veneered with ebony, *c.* 1785; the panels of *pietra dura* probably date from the late 17th century. It was bought in Paris for George IV in 1816

8 French clock by François-Louis Godon, white marble and gilt bronze, carved with figures of Venus and Cupid, 1792

9 Monumental pedestal clock, veneered with tulipwood and fitted with elaborately chased gilt and patinated bronze mounts. Although stamped by Duhamel (active 1750-1801) it was probably made in the 1730s, possibly by Jean-Pierre Latz. Bought by George IV in 1816, it was placed at the foot of the staircase in Carlton House, London

PORCELAIN

10 Dark blue Chinese porcelain vases with French gilt bronze mounts in the Louis XV and Louis XVI styles, 18th century

THE EAST GALLERY

PICTURES

11 Studio of Sir Peter Paul Rubens: *The Family of Balthasar Gerbier, c.1630*

12 John Russell: *George, Prince of Wales* (later George IV), 1791; the Prince is in the uniform of the Royal Kentish Bowmen

13 Franz Xaver Winterhalter: *The Family of Queen Victoria*, 1846

14 John Hoppner: *George, Prince of Wales* (later George IV), 1796

15 Benjamin West: *Queen Charlotte*, 1782

16 Benjamin West: *Prince Adolphus (later Duke of Cambridge), with Princesses Mary and Sophia*, 1778

17 Benjamin West: *George III*, 1779

18 John Hoppner: *Francis, 5th Duke of Bedford, c.1797*

19 Sir George Hayter: *The Coronation of Queen Victoria*, 1838

20 John Hoppner: *Francis, 5th Earl of Moira and 1st Marquess of Hastings, c.1793*

21 Sir Joshua Reynolds: *Frederick, Duke of York*, 1785

FURNITURE

22 Large clock signed by the Parisian bronze manufacturer De La Croix, gilt and patinated bronze, c.1775; the dial is a later insertion by Vulliamy

23 Two pairs of candelabra by Pierre-Philippe Thomire, gilt bronze supported by figures of patinated bronze, c.1810; they entered the collection in 1813. They stand on ebony and brass pedestals, French, early 19th century

THE CROSS GALLERY

PICTURES

24 Benjamin West: *The Departure of Regulus*, 1769; formerly hung in George III's Warm Room at Buckingham House before its transformation by George IV

25 Benjamin West: *The Oath of Hannibal*, 1770

THE WEST GALLERY

TAPESTRIES

26 Four tapestries woven at the Gobelins manufactory from a series of 28 illustrating the exploits of Don Quixote, second half of the 18th century; given to George IV by the artist Richard Cosway

FURNITURE

27 Boulle knee-hole desk, veneered with tortoise-shell, ebony and brass, late 17th century

28 Chairs designed by Robert Jones and made by Tatham, Bailey & Sanders, gilded wood, 1823; made for the Saloon, the Royal Pavilion, Brighton

PORCELAIN

29 Two oriental porcelain vases on marble pedestals with mounts by the Vulliamys, 1808-14

RIGHT: *Monumental pedestal clock possibly by Jean-Pierre Latz*, 1730s

THE STATE DINING ROOM was originally intended to be a Music Room. The pair of white marble chimney-pieces, possibly the work of Matthew Cotes Wyatt, show flanking female figures playing musical instruments and indicate the original intended function of the room. It is possible that the bed of the ceiling with its three little saucer domes may also have been designed by Nash as it is more refined than the coving of Blore's surround with its heavy and restless bracketing.

One of a set of four five-light gilt bronze candelabra on red marble bases made for the comte d'Artois's apartments at Versailles in 1783

Sir Thomas Lawrence and studio: King George IV in his Coronation robes, c. 1820

The room was completed as a dining room for William IV and Queen Victoria, both of whose cyphers can be found in the plaster roundels in the penetration of the coving. The pier glasses, pelmets and other florid gilded enrichments of the room were designed by Blore. The principal feature of the room is the series of splendid, full-length royal portraits. The alcove at the south end, which now contains the entrance to the West Gallery, was originally the sideboard recess, used for displaying gold plate during banquets, but was altered when Pennethorne's wing was added in 1853-5.

A great feature of the State Dining Room and all the rooms on the west side of the palace are the beautiful views over the gardens landscaped in the 1820s for George IV by Nash and William Townsend Aiton, the head gardener at Kew; the lake and picturesque, naturalistic planting of trees and shrubs, and green lawns make the palace truly *rus in urbe*. The gardens form the setting for the summer garden parties, originally started by Queen Victoria when they were called 'breakfasts' despite taking place in the afternoon, and revived by George VI. These have become an increasingly popular feature of the Buckingham Palace year.

Gilt bronze and marble clock by Pierre-Philippe Thomire, bought by George IV in 1810

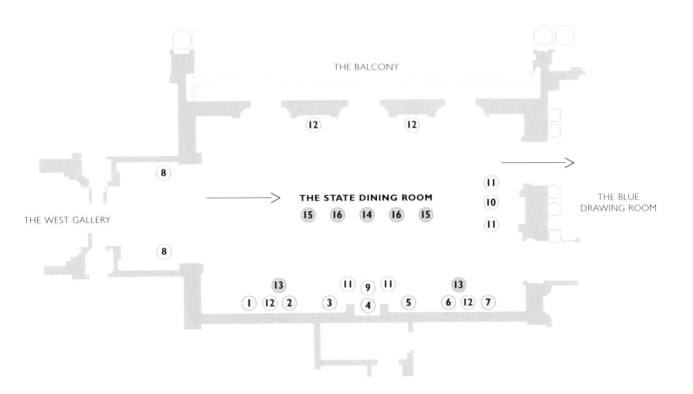

THE BALCONY

⑫   ⑫

⑧

THE STATE DINING ROOM
⑮ ⑯ ⑭ ⑯ ⑮

⑪
⑩
⑪

THE BLUE
DRAWING ROOM

THE WEST GALLERY

⑧

⑬   ⑪ ⑨ ⑪   ⑬
① ⑫ ②   ③   ④   ⑤   ⑥ ⑫ ⑦

PICTURES

The display illustrates the development of state portraiture during the second half of the 18th century.

1 Sir Godfrey Kneller: *Caroline, Princess of Wales* (later Queen, wife of George II), 1716

2 Jean-Baptiste van Loo: *Frederick, Prince of Wales*, 1742

3 Allan Ramsay: *Queen Charlotte* (wife of George III), *c.* 1763

4 Studio of Sir Thomas Lawrence: *George IV, c.* 1820

5 Allan Ramsay: *George III, c.* 1763

6 Jean-Baptiste van Loo: *Augusta, Princess of Wales* (wife of Frederick, Prince of Wales), 1742

7 Studio of John Shackleton: *George II*, 1755-7

FURNITURE

8 Pair of candelabra by Thomire & Cie, malachite and gilt bronze, *c.* 1828

9 Clock by Benjamin Vulliamy, marble and gilt bronze, fitted with three porcelain figures by William Duesbury of Derby, 1788; designed for the Prince of Wales (later George IV)

10 Clock by Pierre-Philippe Thomire, gilt bronze and marble, representing Apollo in his chariot drawn by four horses, early 19th century; bought by George IV in 1810, its movement was changed by Benjamin Lewis Vulliamy in 1834

11 Set of four five-light candelabra by François Rémond, gilt bronze on red marble bases, 1783; made for the closet decorated in the Turkish manner in the comte d'Artois'

apartments at Versailles. Bought by George IV in 1820

12 Set of parcel gilt mahogany sideboards with gilt bronze and glass backs, 1838

PORCELAIN

13 Chinese celadon porcelain vases with French and English gilt bronze mounts, 18th and early 19th century; most of these were at the Royal Pavilion, Brighton in the early 19th century

TABLE SILVER

14 Oval tureen, cover and stand by Paul Storr, silver gilt, 1812; made for George IV

15 Pair of ewers and stands by Rundell, Bridge & Rundell, silver gilt, 1822; made for George IV

16 Pair of wine bottle coolers by Digby Scott and Benjamin Smith, silver gilt, 1803; made for George IV

GUESTS GATHER HERE FOR drinks before large luncheon parties and grand state and diplomatic occasions. This is one of the finest rooms in the palace and the *ne plus ultra* of Georgian sumptuousness in decoration, even more splendid than the Throne Room sequence on the east front. It is 68 feet long and divided into bays by giant Corinthian columns. It was first called the South Drawing Room and its original decoration was a symphony of red with *Porfido rosso* porphyry scagliola columns, crimson velvet curtains and figured silk wall hangings. It now has a blue flock paper installed by Queen Mary at the beginning of the century, while

The 'Table of the Grand Commanders', a gift from Louis XVIII to George IV in 1817

Sèvres porcelain vase, c. 1770.

the Corinthian columns were painted to resemble onyx to cover up defects in the scagliola, in the reign of Queen Victoria. The ceiling, with its great billowing coves and bold console brackets shows Nash at his most daring and most original.

The three moulded plaster reliefs in the tympana are by William Pitts (1835) and have a literary theme depicting the *Apotheoses of Shakespeare* (north), *of Spenser* (south) and *of Milton* (facing north). The florid whiteness of the forms and foliage stands out against a richly gilded ground. This, and the following two rooms are the principal features of Buckingham Palace. The richness of their fittings and fixtures

distinguishes them from any comparable state rooms in England, while the originality of their architecture marks them out from contemporary palace rooms on the Continent. The aim of George IV and Nash, in which they triumphantly succeeded, was to create an aura of extreme opulence.

Marble and gilt bronze astronomical clock with three dials by Jean Antoine Lépine, c. 1790.

THE GARDEN

④

⑤   ④
          ③⑤
⑧   ⑧   ⑨

THE STATE DINING → | THE BLUE DRAWING ROOM | THE MUSIC ROOM
ROOM

⑥   ⑧   ⑧   ⑨
                        ③⑤
⑤   ③   ④
④   ③   ③   ⑨
          ⑨   ⑨
          ①   ⑦   ②

PICTURES

1 Sir Luke Fildes; *George V*, 1911-12
2 Sir William Llewellyn: *Queen Mary*, 1911-13

FURNITURE

3 Set of four side tables by Alexandre-Louis.
   Bellangé, marble and gilt bronze, 1823;
   bought by George IV in 1825 for Windsor
   Castle

4 Part of a set of settees and armchairs by
   Tatham, Bailey and Sanders, c. 1810

5 Two pairs of candelabra attributed to
   François Rémond, gilt bronze, incorporating a
   flaming torch and chains hung from eagles'
   heads, c. 1787; probably acquired by
   George IV for Carlton House, London, in the
   1780s. There are two further pairs in the
   Music Room

6 'Table of the Grand Commanders', hard-paste
   Sèvres porcelain with gilt bronze mounts,
   1806-12. The table-top is painted by Louis-
   Bertin Parant with the head of Alexander the
   Great (centre) surrounded by the heads of 12

other commanders from antiquity, all in
imitation of cameo reliefs. The mounts are
by Pierre-Philippe Thomire. Commissioned
by Napoleon in 1806, it was presented to
King George IV by Louis XVIII in 1817; the gift
so delighted the Prince Regent, as he then
was, that Sir Thomas Lawrence was
instructed to include it henceforth in all
official portraits; one version is in the State
Dining Room

7 Astronomical clock with three dials by Jean-
   Antoine Lépine, marble and gilt bronze,
   c.1790;. bought by George IV in 1790

8 Set of four cut glass chandeliers, English,
   c. 1810

PORCELAIN

9 Vases, Sèvres porcelain painted with a dark
   blue ground, second half of the 18th century;
   they include some rare models of ambitious
   design

ORIGINALLY KNOWN AS THE Bow Drawing Room, this occupies the centre of the garden front behind the semi-circular bow window which was an architectural feature much admired by George IV. It is more disciplined than the Blue Drawing Room with an ingeniously designed, almost Soanic vaulted and domed ceiling, all lavishly gilded. This is the room where guests, having assembled in the Green Drawing Room are presented before a dinner or a banquet. Here too, royal babies are sometimes christened. The Queen's three eldest children were all baptised here in water brought from the River Jordan.

A spectacular feature of the room is the parquet floor of satinwood, rosewood, tulipwood, mahogany, holly and other woods. It was made by Thomas Seddon and cost £2,400. It is a triumph of English craftsmanship, and one of the finest of its type in the country. The columns round the wall are of lapis lazuli scagliola, and originally the walls were hung with bright yellow silk which must have presented a dramatic visual impact in conjunction with the blue columns. In the tympana at the tops of the walls are three graceful reliefs by William Pitts depicting the *Progress of Rhetoric*. The subjects are *Harmony* (north), *Eloquence* (east) and *Pleasure* (south). Over the white marble fireplaces are large arched mirrors in concave plaster frames designed by Nash which complete the architectural treatment of the room.

THE ROYAL FAMILY GATHER here before meeting their guests in the Music Room. This was originally called the North Drawing Room and the pilasters were of Siena scagliola and the walls covered with gold and white figured damask. The present white and gold French-inspired wall decoration dates from the late nineteenth century. The ceiling survives as designed by Nash and combines a swagger tent-like composition with brilliant convex coving and delicate moulded plaster-work by Bernasconi.

William Pitts' twelve frieze panels depict the *Origin and Progress of Pleasure* and were described by the Parliamentary Select Committee into the financing of the rebuilding in 1831 as the 'sports of Boys'; they cost £800. The twelve individual panels are *Love Awakening the Soul to Pleasure*; the *Soul in the Bower of Fancy*; the *Pleasure of Decoration*; the *Invention of Music*; the *Pleasure of Music*; the *Dance*; the *Masquerade*; the *Drama*; the *Contest for the Palm*; the *Palm Assigned*; the *Struggle for the Laurel*; the *Laurel Obtained*. The two white marble chimney-pieces after a design by Flaxman are particularly fine. The gilt framed pier glasses were designed by Blore. One of them conceals a secret door from the Royal Closet through which the Royal Family enters the state apartments on formal occasions. The capitals of the pilasters were designed by Nash and are a novel composition incorporating the Garter star.

Roll top desk by Jean-Henri Riesener veneered with fret marquetry and inlaid with trophies and flowers. Purchased by George IV in 1825

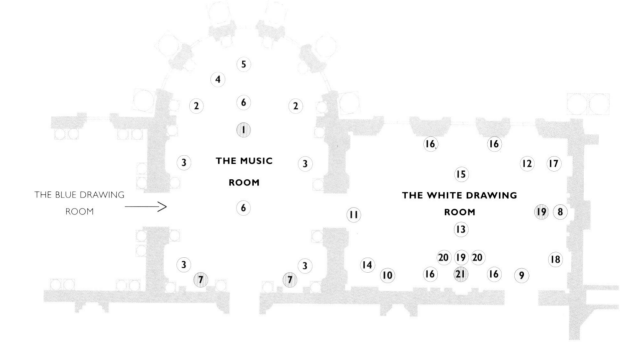

THE MUSIC ROOM

FITTINGS

1 Marquetry floor, satinwood, holly and other woods inlaid with the cypher of George IV, 1831; it cost £2,400

FURNITURE

2 Throne chairs of George V and Queen Mary, when Prince and Princess of Wales, used during the Coronation of Edward VII in 1902

3 Small armchairs and settees by Georges Jacob, c. 1786; imported into England by Dominique Daguerre in the late 1780s for Carlton House, London

4 Grand piano by John Broadwood & Sons, 20th century

5 Vase by Pierre-Philippe Thomire, patinated and gilt bronze, early 19th century; bought by George IV in 1812

6 Pair of English chandeliers, cut glass and gilt bronze, early 19th century

PORCELAIN

7 Vases, soft-paste Sèvres porcelain; those on the left-hand chimney-piece form a garniture, 1764

THE WHITE DRAWING ROOM

PICTURES

8 François Flameng: *Queen Alexandra*, 1908

9 After Joseph Vivien: *François de la Mothe Fénélon, Archbishop of Cambrai*

10 After Sir Anthony van Dyck: *Portrait of a Man in Armour.*

11 Sir Peter Lely: *Portrait of a Lady*, c. 1658-60

FURNITURE

12 Roll-top desk by Jean-Henri Riesener, veneered with fret marquetry and inlaid with trophies, flowers, etc, c. 1775; it may have been made for one of Louis XV's daughters, and at the time of its purchase in 1825 by George IV it was thought to have belonged to Louis XVI

13 Set of French cabriole-legged armchairs by Jean-Baptiste Gourdin, mid-18th century

14 Piano by Sébastien and Pierre Erard in a gilded case painted in colours with singeries by Francis Richards, mid-19th century; bought by Queen Victoria in 1856

15 Set of five chandeliers, gilt bronze and cut glass, English, early 19th century

16 Set of four French candelabra, gilt and patinated bronze, in the form of a faun or nymph holding cornucopia, late 18th century, on gilded wood pedestals supplied by Tatham, Bailey and Sanders, 1811; made for Carlton House, London

17 Pair of candelabra, by Pierre-Philippe Thomire, gilt bronze, the candle-arms in the form of bugles attached to a central shaft which spring from a military trophy, early 19th century; bought by George IV in 1813

18 Pair of French gilt bronze candelabra, late 18th century

19 French patinated and gilt bronze and white marble mantel clock, late 18th century

20 Pair of French patinated and gilt bronze candelabra, late 18th century

PORCELAIN

21 Vases, Sèvres porcelain, second half of the 18th century

THE MINISTERS' STAIRS at the north end of the Picture Gallery lead down to the ground floor. They were introduced in 1834 by Blore to improve the circulation of this end of the palace. They have a gilt lead balustrade of simpler design than that on the Grand Stairs. At its foot is a white marble group by Antonio Canova depicting Mars and Venus which was commissioned by George IV (when Prince Regent) for the conservatory at Carlton House (c. 1817–18).

ABOVE: *Barograph in mahogany and gilt bronze. Commissioned by George III in 1765*

LEFT: *Mars and Venus by Antonio Canova. Commissioned by George IV in 1815*

THE MARBLE HALL lies underneath the Picture Gallery running from north to south of the main block. It was originally conceived, at Lord Farnborough's suggestion, as a Sculpture Gallery, repeating the arrangement in his house at Bromley Hill, Kent, which had separate sculpture and picture galleries super-imposed. Its original architectural character was more austere with plain scagliola walls as a background to marble statues. The floor and Corinthian columns are of Carrara marble and match those in the Grand Hall, to which it is spatially connected. The two small-scale marble chimney-pieces were probably brought from Carlton House when it was demolished. Here, as elsewhere, the later gilded decorations were added by Bessant in 1902; the carved and gilded wood swags above the fireplaces which may be in part late seventeenth-century in date, were placed here then.

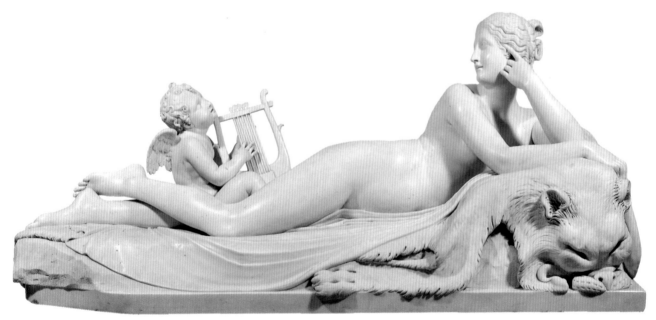

TOP: *Franz Xaver Winterhalter:* Queen Victoria *and* Prince Albert, *1859*

ABOVE: *Antonio Canova:* Fountain Nymph with Putto, *1817-18*

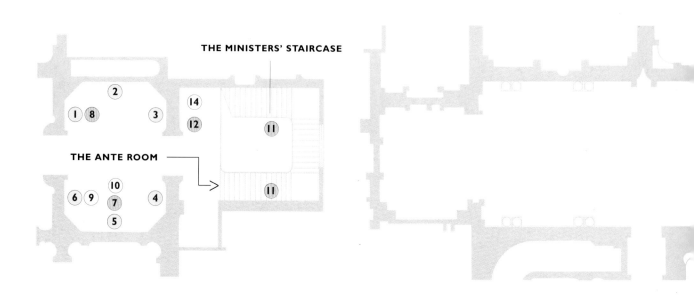

THE MINISTERS' STAIRCASE

THE ANTE ROOM

THE GRAND HALL

THE ANTE ROOM

PICTURES

1 Heinrich von Angeli: *Princess Victoria Mary of Teck (later Queen Mary)*, 1893

2 Karl Schmidt of Bamberg after Winterhalter: *Prince Albert*, painted on porcelain, 2nd half of the 19th century

3 Heinrich von Angeli: *Princess Beatrice, Princess Henry of Battenberg*, 1893

4 Heinrich von Angeli: *Princess Helena, Princess Christian of Schleswig-Holstein*, 1875

5 Edward Hughes: *Mary, Duchess of York (later Queen Mary)*, 1895

6 Heinrich von Angeli: *Princess Louise, Marchioness of Lorne*, 1875

SCULPTURE

7 W. Reid Dick: *Bust of Queen Mary*, bronze, 1938

8 Harry O'Hanlon: *Family of the Horse*, bronze, 1988; presented to H.M. The Queen in 1990

9 M. Moch: *Two loons (Canadian sea birds)*; green soapstone, 1990; presented to H.M. The Queen by the Prime Minister of Canada during the 1990 State Visit

FURNITURE

10 Spanish damascened steel table made by Placido Zuloaga for Alfred Morrison, 1880; purchased for the Royal Collection by Queen Elizabeth in 1938

THE MINISTERS' STAIRCASE

TAPESTRIES

11 Two panels from a set of four, *Les Amours des Dieux*, woven at the Gobelins manufactury after designs by Joseph-Marie Vien, late 18th century; bought by George IV in 1826

SCULPTURE

12 Mowlm: *Five Inouits Tossing a child*: green soapstone, 1977; a Jubilee present to H.M. The Queen

13 Antonio Canova: *Mars and Venus*, c. 1815-17; commissioned by George IV following Canova's visit to England in 1815, it was delivered to Carlton House, London, in 1824, where it was placed in the Gothic Conservatory

FURNITURE

14 Barograph by Alexander Cumming, mahogany and gilt bronze, 1765; commissioned by George III and delivered to Buckingham House at a cost of £1,178

15 Barometer and Pedestal, attributed to Jean-Pierre Latz, Boulle marquetry and gilt bronze mounts, c. 1735

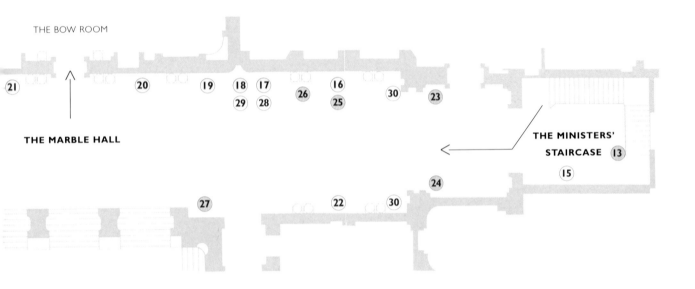

THE BOW ROOM

㉑ ⑳ ⑲ ⑱ ⑰ ㉖ ⑯ ㉚ ㉓
㉙ ㉘ ㉕

THE MARBLE HALL

**THE MINISTERS'
STAIRCASE** ⑬

⑮

㉔

㉗ ㉒ ㉚

THE MARBLE HALL

PICTURES

The official portraits of Queen Victoria and
Prince Albert dating from 1859 are preceded by
likenesses of their relations.

16 Domenico Pellegrini: *Augustus, Duke of Sussex,*
c. 1804

17 Franz Xaver Winterhalter: *Victoire, Duchess of
Nemours* (cousin of Queen Victoria), 1840

18 George Dawe: *Ernest I, Duke of Saxe-Coburg-
Gotha* (father of Prince Albert), c.1818-19

19 Franz Xaver Winterhalter: *Victoria, Duchess of
Kent* (mother of Queen Victoria), 1849

20 Franz Xaver Winterhalter: *Prince Albert,* 1859;
in the uniform of Colonel of the Rifle Brigade

21 Franz Xaver Winterhalter: *Queen Victoria,*
1859

22 Eduard von Heuss: *Charles, Prince of Leiningen,*
1841

SCULPTURE

23 Nielsine Petersen: *Christian IX, King of
Denmark,* (father of Queen Alexandra), 1906

24 Nielsine Petersen: *Louise, Queen of Denmark,*
(mother of Queen Alexandra), 1906

25 Antonio Canova: *Fountain Nymph with Putto,*
1817-18; commissioned by Earl Cawdor,
who agreed to relinquish his rights to it in
favour of George IV. It reached Carlton House,
London, in 1819

26 John Francis: *Ernest I of Saxe-Coburg-Gotha*
(father of Prince Albert), 1846

27 Emil Wolff: *Sea Nymph with Trident,* 1841

FURNITURE

28 A side table by James Moore, gilt gesso,
c. 1715

29 Mantel clock by Benjamin Vulliamy, gilt bronze
and biscuit porcelain, c. 1780

30 Pair of large vases, cloisonné enamel, early
20th century; given to George V and Queen
Mary by the Empress of China on their
Coronation

*Domenico Pellegrini: Augustus, Duke of
Sussex, c. 1804*

THIS ROOM IS WELL-KNOWN to visitors to the garden parties as it is the way they pass into the garden. Its more restrained classical architecture with simple Ionic columns is typical of the semi-state rooms on the ground floor which were originally intended as George IV's private apartments. This was to be the King's library but was never fitted up as such. The pair of dark marble chimney-pieces with Empire gilt bronze mounts by Benjamin Vulliamy date from 1810 and were purchased by Queen Mary and inserted here where they form a sympathetic counterpart to Nash's architecture. The oval portraits with gilt frames set into the walls were installed at the wish of Queen Victoria in 1853.

The Chelsea porcelain service presented by King George III to his brother-in-law, the Duke of Mecklenburg-Strelitz, in 1763

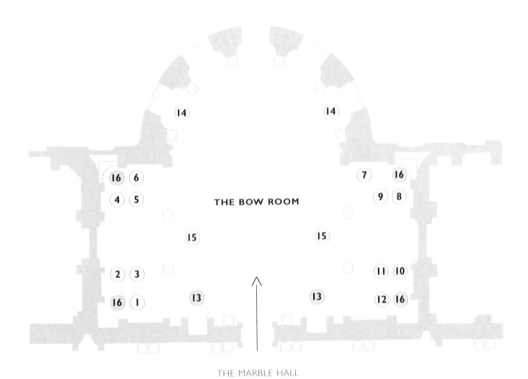

THE BOW ROOM

THE MARBLE HALL

PICTURES

1 Nicaise de Keyser: *Marie Henriette, Duchess of Brabant* (later Queen of the Belgians), 1854

2 Eliseo Sala: *Ferdinand of Savoy, Duke of Genoa*, 1853

3 Frans Xaver Winterhalter: *Augusta, Princess of Prussia* (later Queen of Prussia and German Empress), 1853

4 Franz Xaver Winterhalter: *Ernest, Prince of Hohenlohe-Langenburg*, 1853

5 Frans Xaver Winterhalter: *Prince Leopold* (later Duke of Albany), 1853

6 Nicaise de Keyser: *Leopold, Duke of Brabant* (later Leopold II, King of the Belgians), 1854

7 Carl Oesterley: *George V, King of Hanover*, 1853

8 Franz Xaver Winterhalter: *Frederick William, Grand Duke of Mecklenburg-Strelitz*, 1853

9 Alexander Melville after Winterhalter: *Princess Augusta of Cambridge, Grand Duchess of Mecklenburg-Strelitz*, 1853

10 Alexander Melville after Winterhalter: *George, Duke of Cambridge*, 1852

11 William Corden after Winterhalter: *Princess Mary Adelaide of Cambridge* (later Duchess of Teck), 1847

12 Carl Ferdinand Sohn: *Maria Alexandrina, Queen of Hanover*, 1853

FITTINGS

13 Two chimney-pieces by Benjamin Vulliamy, black marble with gilt bronze mounts, 1810; commissioned by the Earl of Bridgwater; they were acquired by George V and Queen Mary

FURNITURE

14 Pair of English incense burners, mahogany in the form of a covered urn on a pedestal, late 18th century; bought by Queen Mary

15 Pair of Regency inkstands, kingwood and gilt bronze, early 19th century

PORCELAIN

16 Service, Chelsea porcelain, 1763; presented by George III and Queen Charlotte to the Queen's brother, Duke Adolphus Frederick IV of Mecklenburg-Strelitz; presented in 1947 to Queen Elizabeth by James Oakes

THE GARDENS OF Buckingham Palace, based on the original plans drawn up by William Townsend Aiton of Kew Gardens and John Nash, provide a walled oasis in the middle of London.

The Queen's Gallery is built on the site of the private chapel, destroyed by the bomb damage to Buckingham Palace in World War II. Each year major exhibitions are open to the public. This year's exhibition is devoted to Fabergé.

The Royal Mews, designed by Nash for George IV, are still in daily use. Constructed around a quad-rangle, the Mews houses the horses, including the Greys, and the State Coaches. The most famous of these is the Gold State Coach, designed by Sir William Chambers in 1760 for George III and used at every corona-tion since that of George IV. The Mews are now open to the public.

ACKNOWLEDGEMENTS

Text written by John Martin Robinson
Copyright © 1994 Royal Collection
Enterprises Limited

Photo credits:
All photographs © Her Majesty The Queen except: Title page: Chorley & Handford, pages 2, 9, and 10: Photographers International, page 7: © Camera Press, page 8: © John Stillwell/ Press Association, page 48: © Tim Graham, page 49 © Hulton Picture Library, © Fishmongers' Company, London (Photo: Bridgeman Art Library). Additional room photographs by Derry Moore.

Published by Michael Joseph Limited in association with Royal Collection Enterprises Limited

Penguin Books Limited
27 Wrights Lane, London w8 5tz

Colour reproduction by Saxon Photolitho, Norwich

Printed in Great Britain by Butler & Tanner Ltd, Frome and London

ISBN: 0 7181 3875 9